Contents

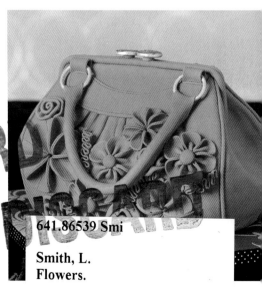

PRICE: $11.50 (3559/he   )

Equipment

For general cake decorating

You will find the following list of general equipment useful when decorating cakes and cookies.

1 Cake boards

Drum – 12mm (½in) thick board to display cakes

Hardboard – a thin strong board, usually the same size as the cake, which is placed under cake to act as a barrier and to give stability to stacked cakes

2 Carving knife – a sharp long-bladed pastry knife, for levelling cakes and carving shapes

3 Cocktail sticks (toothpicks) – used as markers and to transfer small amounts of edible paste colour

4 Dowels – used in conjunction with hardboards to support tiered cakes

5 Measuring spoons – for accurate measurement of ingredients

6 Paintbrushes – a range of sizes is useful for stippling, painting and dusting

7 Paint palette – for mixing edible paste colours and dusts prior to painting and dusting

8 Rolling pin – for rolling out the different types of paste

9 Scissors – for cutting templates and trimming paste to shape

10 Set square – for accurate alignment

11 Spacers – 1.5mm (¹⁄₁₆in) and 5mm (³⁄₁₆in) for rolling out paste

12 Spirit level – to check dowels are vertical and tops of cakes are horizontal

13 Tins (pans) – for baking cakes ball, round and multi-sized

14 Non-stick work board – for rolling out pastes

15 Smoother – to give a smooth and even finish to sugarpaste

16 Sugar shaper and discs – to create pieces of uniformly shaped modelling paste

17 Modelling tools

Ball tool (FMM) – gives even indentations in paste and softens the edges of petals

Craft knife – for intricate cutting tasks

Cutting wheel (PME) – use instead of a knife to avoid dragging the paste

Dresden tool – to create markings on paste

Palette knife – for cutting paste and spreading royal icing

Quilting tool (PME) – for adding stitching lines

Scriber (PME) – for scribing around templates, popping air bubbles in paste and removing small sections of paste

Sugar Recipes

Most of the sugar recipes used in this booklet for covering and decoration can easily be made at home. Use edible paste colours to colour them according to the individual project.

Sugarpaste (rolled fondant)

Used to cover cakes and boards, ready-made sugarpaste can be obtained from major supermarkets and cake-decorating suppliers, and is available in white and the whole colour spectrum. It is also easy and inexpensive to make your own.

Ingredients
Makes 1kg (2¼lb)

★ 60ml (4 tbsp) cold water
★ 20ml (4 tsp/1 sachet) powdered gelatine
★ 125ml (4 fl oz) liquid glucose
★ 15ml (1 tbsp) glycerine
★ 1kg (2¼lb) icing (confectioners') sugar, sifted, plus extra for dusting

tip...

For tips and discussion about making your own sugarpaste, visit the Lindy's Cakes blog.

1 Place the water in a small bowl, sprinkle over the gelatine and soak until spongy. Stand the bowl over a saucepan of hot but not boiling water and stir until the gelatine is dissolved. Add the glucose and glycerine, stirring until well blended and runny.

2 Put the sifted icing (confectioners') sugar in a large bowl. Make a well in the centre and slowly pour in the liquid ingredients, stirring constantly. Mix well.

3 Turn out onto a surface dusted with icing (confectioners') sugar and knead until smooth, sprinkling with extra sugar if the paste becomes too sticky. The paste can be used immediately or tightly wrapped and stored in a plastic bag until required.

Modelling paste

Used to add decoration to cakes, this versatile paste keeps its shape well and dries harder than sugarpaste. Although there are commercial pastes available, it is easy and a lot cheaper to make your own – I always do!

Ingredients
Makes 225g (8oz)

★ 225g (8oz) sugarpaste (rolled fondant)
★ 5ml (1 tsp) gum tragacanth

Make a well in the sugarpaste and add the gum tragacanth. Knead in. Wrap in a plastic bag and allow the gum to work before use. You will begin to feel a difference in the paste after an hour or so, but it is best left overnight. The modelling paste should be firm but pliable with a slight elastic texture. Kneading the modelling paste makes it warm and easy to work with.

Modelling paste tips

★ Gum tragacanth is a natural gum available from cake-decorating suppliers.
★ If time is short use CMC (Tylose) instead of gum tragacanth – this a synthetic alternative but it works almost straight away.
★ Placing your modelling paste in a microwave for a few seconds is an excellent way of warming it for use.
★ If you have previously added a large amount of colour to your paste and it is consequently too soft, an extra pinch or two of gum tragacanth will be necessary.
★ If your paste is crumbly or too hard to work, add a touch of white vegetable fat (shortening) and a little cooled boiled water and knead until softened.

Buttercream

Buttercream is used as a filling between layers of cake, as a glue to attach sugarpaste to cakes and as a topping on cupcakes.

Standard buttercream

Ingredients
Makes 450g (1lb)

★ 110g (3¾oz) unsalted (sweet) butter
★ 350g (12oz) icing (confectioners') sugar
★ 15–30ml (1–2 tbsp) milk or water
★ A few drops of vanilla extract or alternative flavouring

1 Place the butter in a bowl and beat until light and fluffy.

2 Sift the icing (confectioners') sugar into the bowl and continue to beat until the mixture changes colour.

3 Add just enough milk or water to give a firm but spreadable consistency.

4 Flavour by adding the vanilla or alternative flavouring, then store the buttercream in an airtight container until required.

Swiss meringue buttercream

For me, this is the best type of buttercream for cupcakes because it is less sweet and it has a beautiful glossy finish. However be warned, this buttercream is not stable above about 15°C (59°F), so it is not suitable for hot days or warm climates!

Ingredients
Makes 500g (1lb 1½oz)

★ 4 large (US extra large) egg whites
★ 250g (9oz) caster (superfine) sugar
★ 250g (9oz) unsalted (sweet) butter, softened
★ A few drops of vanilla extract

1 Place the egg whites and sugar in a bowl over a saucepan of simmering water. Stir to prevent the egg whites cooking.

2 Once the sugar crystals have dissolved, remove the bowl from the heat and whisk the meringue to its full volume and until the mixture is cool – about five minutes.

3 Add the butter and vanilla and continue to whisk for about 10 minutes. The mixture will reduce in volume and look curdled – don't panic, just keep whisking until the icing has a smooth, light and fluffy texture.

4 This buttercream is stable at a cool room temperature for a day or two. Store any unused buttercream in a refrigerator and re-beat before using.

Flavouring buttercream

Try replacing the liquid in the recipes with:

★ Alcohols such as whisky, rum or brandy
★ Other liquids such as coffee, melted chocolate, lemon curd or fresh fruit purees
★ Or add:
★ Nut butters to make a praline flavour
★ Flavours such as mint or rose extract

Flower paste

Available commercially from sugarcraft suppliers, flower paste (also known as petal or gum paste) is used to make delicate sugar flowers and has been used in the Perfect Poppies and the Maroon Bloom projects in this booklet. Flowers made from flower paste retain their shape and are not as badly affected by moisture as flowers made from other pastes. This paste can be bought in white and a variety of colours. There are many varieties available so try a few to see which you prefer. Alternatively, it is possible to make your own, but it is a time-consuming process and you will need a heavy-duty mixer.

Ingredients
Makes 500g (1lb 2oz)

★ 500g (1lb 2oz) icing (confectioners') sugar
★ 15ml (1 tbsp) gum tragacanth
★ 25ml (1½ tbsp) cold water
★ 10ml (2 tsp) powdered gelatine
★ 10ml (2 tsp) liquid glucose
★ 15ml (1 tbsp) white vegetable fat (shortening)
★ 1 medium egg white

1 Sieve the icing (confectioners') sugar and gum tragacanth into the greased mixing bowl of a heavy-duty mixer (the grease eases the strain on the machine).

2 Place the water in a small bowl, sprinkle over the gelatine and soak until spongy. Stand the bowl over a saucepan of hot but not boiling water and stir until the gelatine is dissolved. Add the glucose and white vegetable fat (shortening) to the gelatine and continue heating until all the ingredients are melted and mixed.

3 Add the glucose mixture and egg white to the icing (confectioners') sugar. Beat the mixture very slowly until mixed – at this stage it will be a beige colour – then increase the speed to maximum until the paste becomes white and stringy.

4 Grease your hands and remove the paste from the bowl. Pull and stretch the paste several times, and then knead together. Place in a plastic bag and store in an airtight container. Leave the paste to mature for at least 12 hours.

Flower paste tips
★ Flower paste dries quickly so when using, cut off only as much as you need and reseal the remainder.
★ Work it well with your hands – it should 'click' between your fingers when it is ready to use.
★ If it is too hard and crumbly, add a little egg white and white vegetable fat (shortening) – the fat slows down the drying process and the egg white makes it more pliable.

Pastillage

This paste is used to make sugar pieces that extend above or to the side of a cake and also to make sugarcraft moulds. It is an extremely useful paste because, unlike modelling paste, it sets extremely hard and is not affected by moisture the way other pastes are. However, the paste crusts quickly and is brittle once dry. You can buy it in a powdered form, to which you add water, but it is easy to make yourself.

Ingredients
Makes 350g (12oz)

★ 1 egg white
★ 300g (11oz) icing (confectioners') sugar, sifted
★ 10ml (2 tsp) gum tragacanth

1 Put the egg white into a large mixing bowl. Gradually add enough icing (confectioners') sugar until the mixture combines together into a ball. Mix in the gum tragacanth and then turn the paste out onto a work board or work surface and knead well.

2 Incorporate the remaining icing (confectioners') sugar into the pastillage to give a stiff paste. Store in a plastic bag placed in an airtight container in a refrigerator for up to one month.

Royal icing

Royal icing is used in several of the projects in this booklet, and below are recipes for two methods for making it.

Quick royal icing

This is a very quick method, which is ideal if time is short or you just wish use a stencil.

Ingredients
- ★ 1 large (US extra large) egg white
- ★ 250g (9oz) icing (confectioners') sugar, sifted

Put the egg white in a bowl, lightly beat to break it down then gradually beat in the icing sugar until the icing is glossy and forms soft peaks.

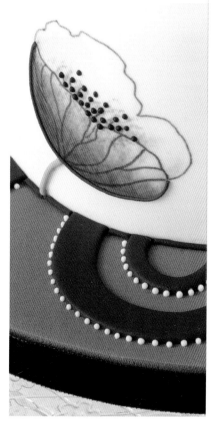

Professional royal icing

This is a more involved method that gives you a better quality of icing, ideal for finer details. Make sure all your equipment is spotless, as even small residues of grease will affect the icing.

Ingredients
- ★ 90g (3oz) egg white (approx 3 eggs or equivalent of dried albumen)
- ★ 455g (1lb) icing (confectioners') sugar, sifted
- ★ 5–7 drops of lemon juice (if using fresh eggs)

1 Separate the egg whites the day before needed, sieve through a fine sieve or tea strainer, cover and then place in a refrigerator to allow the egg white to strengthen.

2 Place the egg whites into the bowl of a mixer, stir in the icing (confectioners') sugar and add the lemon juice.

3 Using the whisk attachment, beat as slowly as possible for between 10 and 20 minutes until the icing reaches soft peaks. How long it takes will depend on your mixer. Take care not to over mix – test by lifting a little icing out of the bowl. If the icing forms a peak that bends over slightly, it is the correct consistency.

4 Store in an airtight container, cover the top surface with cling film (plastic wrap) and then a clean damp cloth to prevent the icing forming a crust, before adding the lid and placing in a refrigerator.

Sugar glue

You can often just use water to stick your sugar decorations to your cakes, however if you find you need something a little stronger try using sugar glue, which is a quick, easy, instant glue to make.

Break up pieces of white modelling paste into a small container and cover with boiling water. Stir until dissolved or to speed up the process place in a microwave for 10 seconds before stirring. This produces a thick strong glue, which can be easily thinned by adding some more cooled boiled water.

White vegetable fat (shortening)

This is a solid white vegetable fat (shortening) that is often known by a brand name: in the UK, Trex or White Flora; in South Africa, Holsum; in Australia, Copha; and in America, Crisco. These products are more or less interchangeable in cake making.

Pretty Pastels

ADDING FABRIC-EFFECT BLOSSOMS
TO CUPCAKES

Arrange fabric-effect
blossoms in groups
of three to create this
sweet and simple
cupcake design.

You will need

- ★ Cupcakes baked in floral paper cases

- ★ Sugarpaste: pink

- ★ Modelling paste: deep pink, purple, aqua

- ★ Crown embosser set (PC)

- ★ Medium oval cutters set 2 (LC)

- ★ Round pastry cutter, same size as cupcakes

- ★ Basic equipment (see page 2)

1 Roll out the pink sugarpaste and, if desired, add a pattern to it by gently embossing with the fancy scroll and heart from the crown set. Cut out a disc of embossed paste using a pastry cutter of an appropriate size and attach to the top of your cupcake.

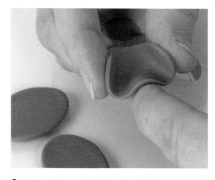

2 To create your fabric-effect blossoms, thinly roll out the modelling paste between narrow spacers and cut out six ovals per flower. Pick up one of the oval shapes, holding it between the thumb and forefinger of one hand, then with your other hand, lift up the centre of one side of the oval.

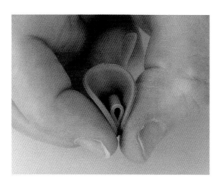

3 Remove your finger from the centre and bring your thumb and forefinger together. Press the paste firmly so the created petal sticks to itself. Repeat for the remaining petals.

4 Using a paintbrush and some sugar glue, stick the petals together to form a circle. Then roll a ball of paste and attach it to the centre of the flower using sugar glue.

5 Repeat the process for additional blooms, then attach your selection of blossoms to your cupcake as desired.

Tender Roses

ADDING FABRIC-EFFECT ROSES
TO CUPCAKES

Fabric-effect roses
created in warm shades
of modelling paste set
the tone for this romantic
cupcake.

You will need

- ★ Cupcakes baked
  in deep pink paper
  cases

- ★ Sugarpaste: ivory

- ★ Modelling paste:
  light pink, dark pink,
  purple

- ★ Textured rolling pins:
  linen look (HP), small
  watermark taffeta
  (HP)

- ★ Cutters: 1.5cm
  (½in) circle, daisy
  marguerites (PME)

- ★ Round pastry
  cutter, same size as
  cupcakes

- ★ Basic equipment
  (see page 2)

1 Roll out the sugarpaste and texture with
a linen-look rolling pin (see box). Cut out
a disc of paste using a pastry cutter of an
appropriate size and attach to the top of
your cupcake.

2 To create your fabric-effect roses, thinly
roll out your modelling paste – if you wish,
texture this with the watermark taffeta rolling
pin. Make sure your paste is firm yet stretchy
– add a little white vegetable fat (shortening)
and/or cooled boiled water if it is a little dry
or doesn't have enough stretch. Fold over a
section of paste and cut the fold to a width of
1.5cm (½in) for a small rose, 7cm (2¾in) for a
large rose or somewhere in between.

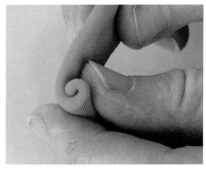

3 Starting at one end of the folded paste, roll
up the paste to form a spiral.

4 Press the cut edges together as you go and gather the paste slightly as you roll to create fullness and space in the flower.

5 Finally, neaten the back of the rose by cutting off the excess paste with scissors. Repeat the process for further roses before attaching them to your cake.

Textured Rolling Pins

A textured rolling pin means that you can easily and speedily add an embossed pattern to a large area of sugarpaste. There are many different sizes and patterns available so chose one that suits your budget and design then use as shown here.

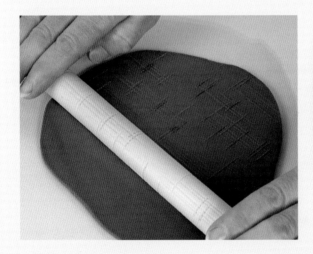

Conventional Use Roll out your sugarpaste or modelling paste, ideally using spacers. Remove the spacers and roll over your paste using your chosen textured rolling pin applying even pressure to give a regular pattern. Try not to re-roll as this can distort the pattern.

Experimental Use Don't be afraid to experiment, for example try over rolling different pins on the same piece of sugarpaste, try varying the pressure to give a textured wave effect or hold one end of the pin while rolling with the other to create a circular pattern.

Darling Dahlia

ADDING FABRIC-EFFECT DAHLIAS TO CUPCAKES

A fabric-effect dahlia made using a small circle cutter adorns this cupcake. Try using modelling paste to tone with the paper cases, or go for greater contrast, as here.

You will need

* ★ Cupcakes baked in purple paper cases

* ★ Sugarpaste: white

* ★ Modelling paste: pink

* ★ Flower embosser (PC cupcake set)

* ★ 24mm (1in) circle cutter (FMM geometric set)

* ★ Quilting tool (PME)

* ★ Round pastry cutter, same size as cupcakes

* ★ Basic equipment (see page 2)

1 Roll out the sugarpaste to a thickness of 5mm (³⁄₁₆in), ideally using spacers, and emboss with the flower cutter-embosser. Cut out a disc of embossed paste using a pastry cutter of an appropriate size and attach to the top of your cupcake.

2 To create your fabric-effect dahlias, thinly roll out modelling paste between narrow spacers and cut out eight circles per flower with the circle cutter. Fold each circle in half and stack the folding circles together using a little sugar glue – don't add too much though as you want the folded paste to stick, not slide.

3 Place the stuck circles on their folds, ease open the stack and bring the two ends together, then glue in place. Adjust the flower so that the petals are evenly spaced.

4 Take a quilting tool and run the wheel down the centre of each petal to add a stitching line. Allow the paste to firm up slightly before adding the flower to your cake.

tip...
Fabric-effect flowers are often made from fabric or leather, but are also highly effective when made from sugar and added to cakes.

Fabric Flowers

The Fuchsia Fashionista project (see page 22) features all of these flowers on a realistic handbag design. Try arrangements of different combinations of flowers to see what different effects can be achieved.

Rose

Blossom

Dahlia

Floral Elegance

ADDING A SIMPLE CUPPED FLOWER TO A CAKE

A simple cupped flower can be made very easily – you just need some modelling paste, a petal cutter, a ball tool and foam pad, and a former. Placed on top of a mini-cake, this flower will transform your cake into a thing of beauty.

You will need

- ★ 5cm (2in) mini-cake

- ★ 10cm (4in) hardboard cake board

- ★ Sugarpaste: coral pink, ivory with a touch of pink

- ★ Modelling paste: coral pink, ivory with a touch of pink

- ★ Textured wallpaper

- ★ Confectioners' glaze

- ★ Ball tool and foam pad

- ★ Cupped former

- ★ Cutters: 2.7cm (1in) wide rose petal (FMM), curled leaf set (LC), small teardrops (LC)

- ★ Piping tube (tip): PME no. 3

- ★ Ivory royal icing

- ★ Piping (pastry) bag

- ★ Narrow cream ribbon

- ★ Basic equipment (see page 2)

1 To create the decorated board using wallpaper, first select the wallpaper you wish to use to emboss the sugarpaste, bearing in mind the scale of your work. Cut the paper to the size of the paste you wish to emboss and seal the textured surface with one or two coats of confectioners' glaze.

tip...

There are many household items that you can use to emboss sugarpaste: spoon handles, buttons, bottle tops, brooches, pan scourers, stiff brushes, lace, wallpaper – anything with a defined pattern on it, provided it is spotlessly clean or can be sealed with a food-grade product such as confectioners glaze.

tip...
Mini-cakes can dry out quickly so try not to
leave them uncovered for any length of time.

2 Cover your cake board with coral pink sugarpaste and trim to size. Place the paper on top of the soft paste and press down firmly in the centre with a smoother. Then, maintaining an even pressure, start to circle the smoother over the back of the paper to transfer the design.

3 Once complete, remove the paper and trim the paste where it has spread slightly over the edge of the board. Leave to dry.

4 To accentuate the embossed design, if desired, mix a contrasting colour of sugarpaste with cooled boiled water until it is a spreadable consistency. Spread this over the board with a palette knife or side scraper then remove the excess using a damp paper towel. Allow to dry.

5 Cover your mini-cake with ivory sugarpaste and allow to dry. Place the cake in the centre of the prepared board.

tip...
Pan scourers make
great tools for
adding subtle texture
to sugarpaste — it
goes without saying
to use only new ones!

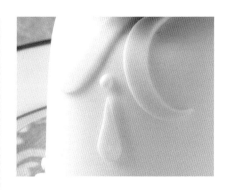

6 Thinly roll out the ivory modelling paste and cut out shapes using the curled leaf and teardrop cutters. Attach these shapes to the cake as desired.

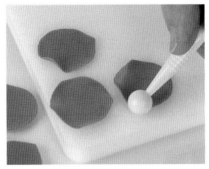

tip...

*If you don't have a
foam pad you can
just use the palm of
your hand.*

7 For the cupped flower, thinly roll out the coral pink modelling paste and cut out a number of petals – how many will depend on the petal cutter you are using and how full you want your flower to appear. In this project I have used six petals.

8 When you use cutters to cut out leaves and petals, there is always a sharp cut edge to remove. Place your petals onto a foam pad then take the ball tool and stroke around the edges of the paste by pressing the tool half on the paste and half on the pad to soften them. To frill the petal edges slightly, push a little more firmly so the paste thins and start to frill.

9 To enable the flower to dry in its cupped shape you will need a former. Ready-made polystyrene formers in a number of sizes are commercially available for this but you can easily make your own former using aluminium foil cupped over the top of a round pastry cutter, cup, glass or any other object with a circular rim.

10 Arrange the petals in the former so that they overlap. Use a touch of sugar glue to secure them in place. To add the flower centre, simply roll lots of modelling paste balls that have been coloured to match the cake and attached these with a little sugar glue.

11 To finish, attach your flower to the top of the mini-cake using a little royal icing then pipe royal icing dots around the lower edge of the cake and on the cake as shown.

Perfect Poppies

ADDING A LIFELIKE POPPY TO A CAKE

I love the brilliance yet simplicity of poppies; their petals may be almost any colour, so can be added to cakes with many different colour schemes. The vivid red sugar poppy in this project is so realistic you would be forgiven for thinking it was a real flower!

You will need

- ★ 12.5cm (5in) round cake
- ★ 13cm (9in) round cake drum
- ★ Sugarpaste: 500g (1lb 2oz) each white, red
- ★ Modelling paste: black, green
- ★ Flower paste: 25g (1oz) red, plus a little black and green
- ★ Edible paste colours: red, black
- ★ Black edible ink pen
- ★ Cutters: large poppy cutter (LC), swirls (PC)
- ★ Poppy petal veiner (GI)
- ★ Sugar shaper
- ★ Piping tube (tip): PME no. 1

- ★ Royal icing: black, white
- ★ Piping (pastry) bags
- ★ Paintbrush and natural sponge
- ★ Flower former
- ★ Paper towel
- ★ Ball tool and foam pad
- ★ Cutting wheel (PME) and tweezers
- ★ 15mm (½in) wide black ribbon
- ★ Basic equipment (see page 2)

1 To make the poppy, thinly roll out the red flower paste and cut out four petals per flower. Place the petals on a foam pad and stroke around the cut edges with a ball tool, half on the paste and half on the pad. Place a petal on top of one half of a double-sided veiner and cover with the second half, making sure it is lined up correctly. Press down firmly to emboss the petal.

2 Release the petal and place into a former. Vein the second petal and place opposite the first in the former. Vein two more petals and place these on top of the first two but at right angles.

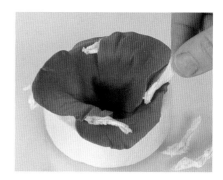

3 Some red poppies have black markings – to add these, dust the base of each petal with black edible dust. Next cut small strips of paper towel, twist and insert between the petals to help give the petals movement and make them look more lifelike.

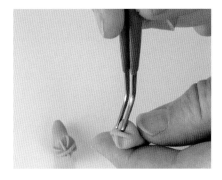

4 To create the flower centre, roll a ball of green flower paste into a cone shape, then using tweezers, pinch eight equal ridges into the top of the cone. Use a Dresden tool to mark light indentations down the cone.

5 To make the stamens, thinly roll out the black flower paste, then using a cutting wheel, make small strokes quickly backwards and forwards through the paste to create a narrow zigzagged cut.

Using sponges with dilute edible paste

Paste colours are concentrated edible colours that are suitable to colour all forms of icing. They can also be diluted with cooled boiled water or clear alcohol (eg gin or vodka) and used as a paint with natural sea sponges to create textured and interesting effects, as shown.

Using a clean damp sponge, blot sections of paint to create a blended appearance. Also try smudging the paint by stroking the paste with the sponge.

6 Cut straight lines on either side of the zigzag to make two separate strips and wrap these around the flower centre. I added two layers to my poppy centre but you could add just one if desired.

7 Cover the cake with white sugarpaste and the cake drum with red sugarpaste (see Covering Cake and Boards) and allow to dry.

8 Dilute red edible paste colour and use the paintbrush to paint five crescent-moon shapes around the side of the cake to create the base of each poppy. Immediately take a damp natural sponge and use to blot the colour into the centre of each flower. See box (left) for further guidance on this technique.

Edible ink pens

Edible ink pens are now widely available in a rainbow of colours, some are even double ended giving you two different tip sizes. The thicker tips are excellent for writing quick messages onto cakes or cookies or filling in shapes with colour, while the fine tips are great for adding fine details or accents to designs. The pens are used in the same way as a standard felt-tip pen and work best when used on light-coloured icing. When working on sugarpaste as shown here, the firmer the surface the easier it is to use the pens.

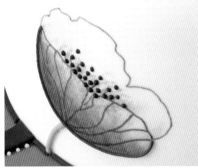

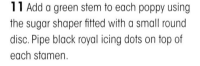

9 Once dry, take the cap off your black edible ink pen and draw the poppy petals and stamens onto your sponge-painted shape (see box above).

10 Add definition to the lower edge of each poppy by adding a thin sausage of black modelling paste made using the sugar shaper (see page 30) fitted with a no. 1 piping tube (tip) instead of a disc.

11 Add a green stem to each poppy using the sugar shaper fitted with a small round disc. Pipe black royal icing dots on top of each stamen.

12 Place the cake on the cake drum, add black modelling paste trim to the join using the sugar shaper, as before.

13 Cut out six large swirls and one small swirl from black modelling paste. Allow to firm slightly then attach one large and the small swirl to the top of the cake. Trim the remaining swirls so they fit neatly around the base of the cake and attach in place.

14 To finish, pipe white royal icing dots around the outside of each swirl.

tip...

PME piping tubes (tips) fit perfectly inside the sugar shaper and give you a smaller hole. The secret is to make sure the paste is very soft.

Maroon Bloom

CREATING A LIFELIKE PEONY CAKE DECORATION

Flamboyant and striking – the king of flowers – the peony is a wonderful bloom to create using flower paste to bring a delicate flourish to your cakes.

You will need

- ★ Flower paste: 150g (5¼oz) claret, 25g (1oz) green

- ★ Edible dust colours: pink (rose SK), purple (violet SK), green

- ★ Large blossom cutter (OP – F6C)

- ★ Random veining tool (HP)

- ★ Ball tool and foam pad

- ★ Peony leaf veiner (GI)

- ★ Flower formers

- ★ Paper towel

- ★ Cutting wheel

- ★ Basic equipment (see page 2)

1 Thinly roll out your claret flower paste and cut out two large five-petal blossoms with the blossom cutter. Take a cutting wheel and remove small 'V' sections of paste from the petal edges as shown. Cover the blossom you are not working on with plastic or a stay-fresh mat to prevent it from drying out.

2 To give the petals some texture and interest, roll over each one with a ceramic veining tool. To do this, place the point of the tool in the centre of the flower and press down gently while rolling the tool in a radial movement across each petal.

3 Place the textured paste onto a foam pad and soften the edges with a ball tool. Hold the tool so it is half on the paste and half on the pad and stroke all the edges – the more pressure you apply, the more movement you will give to the petals.

4 Place one set of petals in a polystyrene cup former then attach the second set of petals to the centre, arranging them so that they rest between the first set. Add space and movement between the petals by inserting small sections of twisted paper towel between the two layers.

5 To create the inside petals, cut five large blossoms from thinly rolled-out flower paste and cover all but one to prevent them drying out. Use the veiner and ball tool as before. Fold the edges of one petal in to the centre then fold again to create tightly curled petals. Add a little sugar glue if necessary but don't press the edges too tightly – you are not trying to stick the petals together, only to give them shape.

6 Repeat for the remaining petals then stand each one up so that they all sit at right angles to the central base of the original blossom.

7 Pinch the paste together at the base of the now vertical petals and place into the centre of the prepared outer petals, attaching with sugar glue. Repeat using the remaining four large blossoms.

Peonies look so effective on cakes in any colour. This pink version provides a pretty flourish.

  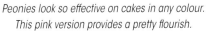

8 Using a Dresden tool, open up and adjust the positioning of the petals to give a natural look. Take a dusting brush and add a little dust colour to the centre of some of the petals to add depth to the flower.

9 Insert sections of twisted paper towel to help the petals stay in position while they dry. Allow the petals to harden but not completely. Remove the peony from its former – the petals should still have a little movement in them not be brittle and hard. If required, add a calyx then place the peony in position on your cake. Add more paper towel if necessary and allow to dry thoroughly.

Fuchsia Fashionista

YOUR FLORAL MASTERPIECE!

Three-dimensional fabric-effect roses, dahlias and blossoms are used, made with techniques demonstrated throughout this booklet, to decorate this gorgeous handbag cake that will make any fashion-conscious woman drool!

You will need

- ★ 25.5cm (10in) square cake

- ★ 25.5cm (10in) square cake drum

- ★ Templates (see pages 25–26)

- ★ Sugarpaste: 600g (1lb 5oz) black, 1kg (2¼lb) deep pink

- ★ Modelling paste: 300g (11oz) deep pink

- ★ Pastillage: 50g (2oz) grey

- ★ Sugar glue

- ★ Edible silver lustre dust (SK)

- ★ White vegetable fat (shortening)

- ★ Confectioners' glaze

- ★ Stencil: crewel ring top design – large 32.5cm (13in) (DS – W086CL)

- ★ Quilting tool (PME)

- ★ Cutters: medium oval cutters set 2 (LC), circle cutters (FMM geometric set)

- ★ Sugar shaper

- ★ Dresden tool

- ★ Craft knife

- ★ Cutting wheel (PME)

- ★ 15mm (½in) wide black-and-white ribbon

- ★ Basic equipment (see page 2)

1 Cover the cake drum with black sugarpaste and add a stencilled pattern with the edible lustre dust, using the technique shown in the box overleaf. Re-trim the board and set aside to dry.

2 Make four pastillage rings using the sugar shaper fitted with the medium round disc (see page 30) and 2.5cm (1in) circle cutter to act as a former. Also make two 2.5cm (1in) round discs for the clasp, embossing the top of each using the stencil. Once completely dry, paint with edible silver lustre dust mixed with confectioners' glaze.

3 Carve the cake using the templates on pages 26, also referring to the tips in the box overleaf. Start by levelling your square cake and cut it in half. Stack the resulting halves to create a 15cm (6in) deep cake. Cut out two of the front templates. Attach one template to either side of your stacked cake using cocktail sticks (toothpicks).

4 Take a large sharp knife and, holding it at right angles to the templates, carve away the excess cake – this gives you the basic handbag outline.

5 Place the overhead template on top of the carved cake and using this as a guide, curve all the corners of the bag using long straight vertical strokes.

Stencilling with Edible Lustre Dust

When using dusts to stencil your cakes and cookies, it is very important to ensure that the products you are using are edible. Read the small print on the pots of dusts that you have to make sure that the ones you are using are not for decoration purposes only. If they are edible they will have an ingredients list and a best before date.

  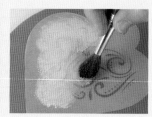 

1 Roll out the sugarpaste to a thickness of 5mm (³⁄₁₆in), ideally using spacers. Place the stencil on top of the sugarpaste. To ensure clean, sharp edges, place a smoother on top of the stencil and press down firmly so that the sugarpaste is forced up to the upper surface of the stencil.

2 Next, smear a thin layer of white vegetable fat (shortening) over the surface of the sugarpaste pattern i.e. the paste that has been forced up through the stencil. Use either a finger or a suitable paintbrush to do this.

3 Take a large, soft dusting brush and dip it into the edible lustre dust, knock off any excess then liberally dust over the stencil, adding more dust as needed. Brush off any excess dust from the stencil – this ensures that as you lift the stencil no stray dust falls from it, spoiling the pattern beneath. Use the brush to burnish the dust (if the product allows) to make it really shine.

4 Carefully lift the stencil away from the paste to reveal the pattern. You may need to use two hands to do this.

6 Remove the templates then mark the central line on the top of the bag where the clasp will be. Using the side template as a guide to the width, mark a line either side of the central line. Cut into the cake along the marked lines to a depth of approximately 1.5cm (½in). Then holding the knife horizontally, cut from the edge of the cake to the vertical cuts just made.

7 Carving the remainder of the cake has to be done freehand. Remove a little cake at a time from the front and back of the bag until you have a curved, shapely bag. The more you take away from the top of the bag, the more slender the bag will look.

8 To shape the sides of the bag, use a small, sharp paring knife. Make a vertical cut at both ends of the clasp section. Then keeping the point of the knife in the cake, cut out a teardrop-shaped wedge of cake from each end. Try and keep the edges of the bag as sharp as possible. Finally round the area below the removed teardrops.

9 Place the carved cake on waxed paper and cover in four sections (see page 28): start by spreading a thin layer of buttercream over the back of the bag.

10 Roll out enough sugarpaste to an even 5mm (³⁄₁₆in) thickness, ideally using spacers, to fit this area roughly. Cut one long edge of the paste straight. Pick up the paste and place on the buttercreamed section so that the cut edge is flush with the lower edge of the cake. Smooth the paste with a smoother to give an even surface.

11 Roughly cut away the excess paste with a pair of scissors – note you are just removing the excess, not trying to give a neat finish. Take a cutting wheel and run it through the sugarpaste to define the side edges of the bag, both sides need to be more or less symmetrical. Then using a craft knife, cut away the excess paste. Cut the paste at the top along the central line.

12 Referring to the front template, add small sausages of sugarpaste to the front of the bag; this will help to give the appearance of pleats. Cover the front of the bag with sugarpaste, cutting to size as for the back. Using your finger and a Dresden tool to shape the sugarpaste over the sausages of paste to look like pleats.

13 Cover both ends of the bag, again cutting one end of the sugarpaste straight before adding the paste to the bag. Trim the paste so it abuts the sugarpaste of the sides.

Tips for Carving Cakes

★ Use a large, sharp pastry knife when carving. If you use a blunt knife it can be hard work, and the cuts you make may not always come away cleanly. You may also find that sections of the cake fall away as you carve which, although they can be repaired, is not ideal.

★ It is much easier to carve a frozen cake than a fresh cake. Freezing allows you to bake the cakes in advance and to carve more intricate shapes without the cake crumbling. It may be necessary to let your cake defrost slightly before carving it.

★ How accurately you carve depends on the shape. With 'organic' shapes it doesn't matter if it's not completely symmetrical, but for some cakes you need to be more exact. Make sure you have a ruler and a set square that starts with zero in the corner, not one with a gap before the measurements start.

14 Use a Dresden tool to blend the joins between the sides and ends of the bag and to create an indention in which the seam trim will sit.

15 Using a sugar shaper, add trim to all the seams using the medium round disc, and to the clasp using the large round disc.

16 Using the template, cut the two curved pieces from thinly rolled modelling paste and attach to the front and back of the bag. Run the quilting tool around each one to create the effect of stitching.

18 Attach the pastillage rings to the top of the bag by looping 2cm (¾in) wide strips of modelling paste through each one and attaching to the top of the curved pieces.

19 Roll two sausages of sugarpaste, 1cm (⅜in) wide by 25cm (10in) long, for the handles. Thinly roll out the remaining modelling paste into a long strip, cut in half lengthways. Wrap each sausage in a strip of modelling paste, so that the modelling paste extends beyond the sausage by approximately 2cm (¾in). Thread these sections of paste through the rings on the bag and fold the paste back on itself to attach the handles. Glue the handles in place, supporting them if necessary while the glue dries.

20 Add small balls of paste to the back of the clasp discs and attach to the top of the bag using sugar glue.

21 Finally, transfer the decorated cake to the prepared board.

17 Make a selection of fabric flowers from modelling paste, following the project steps on pages 7–10. Attach to the front of the bag.

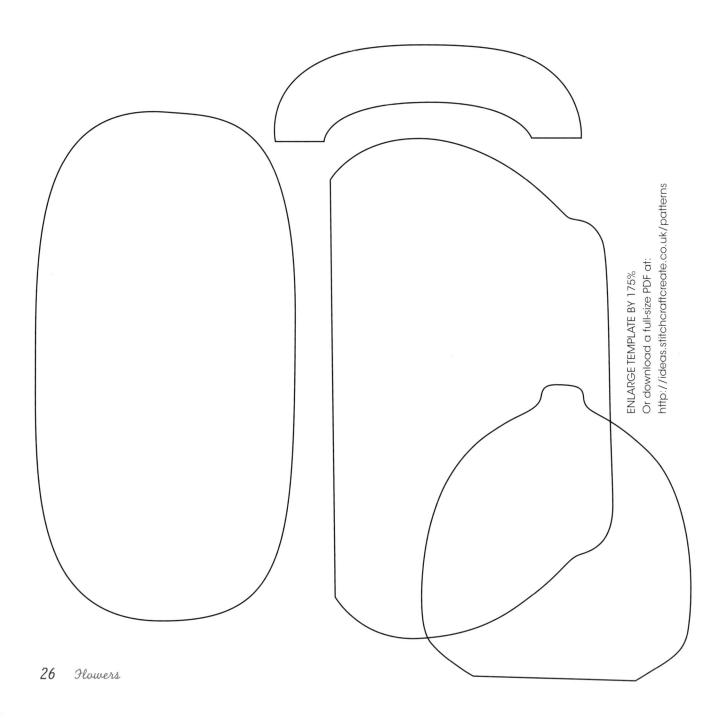

ENLARGE TEMPLATE BY 175%
Or download a full-size PDF at:
http://ideas.stitchcraftcreate.co.uk/patterns

Covering Cakes and Boards

Follow these techniques to achieve a neat and professional appearance to your cakes, cupcakes, cookies and cake boards. With care and practice, you will soon find that you have a perfectly smooth finish.

Levelling the cake

Making an accurate cake base is an important part of creating your masterpiece. There are two ways to do this, depending on the cake:

Method 1 Place a set square up against the edge of the cake and, with a sharp knife, mark a line around the top of the cake at the required height: 7–7.5cm (2–3in). With a large serrated knife cut around the marked line and across the cake to remove the domed crust.

Method 2 Place a cake board into the base of the tin (pan) in which the cake was baked so that when the cake is placed on top, the outer edge of the cake will be level with the tin, and the dome will protrude above. Take a long, sharp knife and cut the dome from the cake, keeping the knife against the tin. This will ensure the cake is completely level.

Sugarpaste quantities

Cake sizes		Sugarpaste quantities – 5mm (³⁄₁₆in) thickness
Round	Square	
7.5cm (3in)		275g (10oz)
10cm (4in)	7.5cm (3in)	350g (12oz)
12.5cm (5in)	10cm (4in)	425g (15oz)
15cm (6in)	12.5cm (5in)	500g (1lb 2oz)
18cm (7in)	15cm (6in)	750g (1lb 10oz)
20cm (8in)	18cm (7in)	900g (2lb)
23cm (9in)	20cm (8in)	1kg (2¼lb)
25.5cm (10in)	23cm (9in)	1.25kg (2¾lb)
28cm (11in)	25.5cm (10in)	1.5kg (3lb)
30cm (12in)	28cm (11in)	1.75kg (3¾lb)
33cm (13in)	30cm (12in)	2kg (4½lb)
35.5cm (14in)	33cm (13in)	2.25kg (4lb 15oz)

Note: These are the amounts of sugarpaste you will need to cover one cake, if you are covering more than one then you will need less than the amounts for each cake added together, as you will be able to reuse the trimmings.

Covering a cake with sugarpaste

1 For a fruit cake, moisten the surface of the marzipan with an even coating of clear spirit, such as gin or vodka, to prevent air bubbles forming under the sugarpaste. For sponge cakes, place the cake on a hardboard cake board the same size as the cake and place on waxed paper. Cover the cake with a thin layer of buttercream to fill in any holes and help the sugarpaste stick to the surface of the cake.

2 Knead the sugarpaste until warm and pliable. Roll out on a surface lightly smeared with white vegetable fat (shortening) rather than icing (confectioners') sugar – fat works well, and you don't have the problems of icing sugar drying out or marking the sugarpaste. Roll out the paste to a depth of 5mm (³⁄₁₆in) using spacers to ensure an even thickness (**A**).

3 Lift the paste carefully over the top of the cake, supporting it with a rolling pin, and position it so that it covers the cake (**B**). Using a smoother, smooth the top surface of the cake to remove any lumps and bumps. Smooth the top edge using the palm of your hand. Always make sure your hands are clean and dry with no traces of cake crumbs before smoothing sugarpaste.

4 Using a cupped hand and an upward movement, encourage the sugarpaste on the sides of the cake to adjust to the shape of your cake (**C**). Do not press down on any pleats in the paste, instead open them out and redistribute the paste, until the cake is completely covered. Smooth the sides using a smoother.

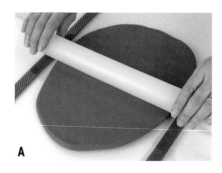

A

B

C

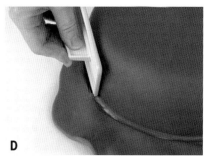

D

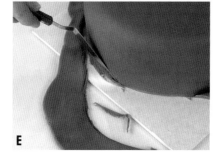

E

F

5 Take the smoother and while pressing down, run the flat edge around the base of the cake to create a cutting line (**D**). Trim away the excess paste with a palette knife (**E**) to create a neat, smooth edge (**F**).

Covering boards

Covering a board with sugarpaste gives you a canvas on which to add decoration to complement and enhance your cake design.

1 Roll out the sugarpaste to a thickness of 4mm (⅛in) or 5mm (³⁄₁₆in) using spacers.

tip...
If you have air bubbles under the icing, insert a scriber or clean glass-headed dressmakers' pin at an angle and press out the air.

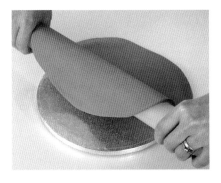

2 Moisten the board with cooled boiled water or sugar glue. Lift up the paste and drape over the board.

3 Circle a smoother over the paste to achieve a smooth, flat finish to the board.

4 Cut the paste flush with the sides of the board using a cranked handled palette knife, taking care to keep the edge vertical. The covered board should ideally be left overnight to dry thoroughly.

Covering mini-cakes

Mini-cakes are covered in exactly the same way as standard cakes, it is just the scale that is different. You will find that the icing pleats more readily so remember to keep opening the pleats (**A**) before smoothing to shape (**B**). You may also find that the sugarpaste is thicker at the bottom of the cake than the top – to help overcome this problem, rotate the cake between to two flat-edged smoothers to help redistribute the paste and ensure the sides of the cake are vertical (**C**).

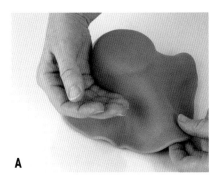

A

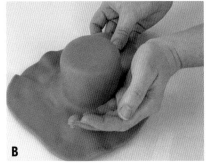

B

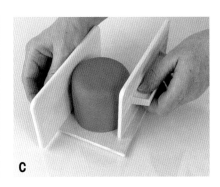

C

Covering cupcakes

It is worth doing a little preparation before covering your cupcakes. Not all cupcakes come out of the oven perfect, some may need a little trimming with a sharp knife while others benefit from a little building up with an appropriate icing.

1 Check each of your cupcakes to ensure that the decoration is going to sit just as you want it to and remedy any that aren't quite right.

2 The sugarpaste may need a little help to secure it to the cupcakes, so brush the cakes with an appropriate syrup or alcohol or add a thin layer of buttercream or ganache, this also adds flavour and interest to the cakes.

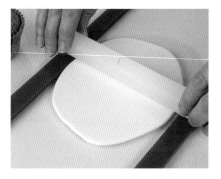

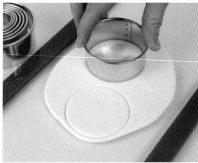

3 Knead the sugarpaste until warm and pliable. Roll out on a surface lightly smeared with white vegetable fat (shortening), rather than icing (confectioners') sugar. Roll out the paste to a depth of 5mm (³⁄₁₆in). It is a good idea to use spacers for this, as they ensure an even thickness.

4 Cut out circles of sugarpaste using an appropriately sized cutter. The size of the circle required will be dependant on the cupcake pan and case used and the amount the cakes have domed.

5 Using a palette knife, carefully lift the paste circles onto each cupcake. Use the palm of your hand to shape the paste to the cupcake, easing the fullness in if necessary.

Using a sugar shaper

This is a fantastic tool – also often known as a clay gun, sugarcraft gun or craft gun The patented pump action of the sugar shaper gives mechanical assistance to squeeze out pastes in various shapes and sizes.

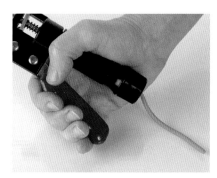

1 Add a little white vegetable fat (shortening) to the paste to stop it getting too sticky (note if too much is added the paste will not harden). Dunk the paste into some cooled boiled water and knead. Repeat until the paste feels soft and stretchy.

2 Insert the softened paste into the barrel of the sugar shaper, then add the required disc and reassemble the tool.

3 Push the plunger down to expel the air and pump the handle to build up pressure, until it 'bites'. The paste should squeeze out easily and smoothly – if it does not the consistency is probably incorrect so remove the paste and add some more fat (shortening) and/or water.

Storage

The following conditions will affect your decorated cakes.
It is therefore best to protect them as much as possible.

★ Sunlight will fade and alter the colours of icing, so always store in a dark place.

★ Humidity can have a disastrous effect on modelling paste and pastillage decorations, causing the icing to become soft and to droop if free standing. It can also causes dark colours to bleed into lighter colours and silver decorations, whether edible or not, to tarnish.

★ Heat can melt icing, especially buttercream, and can prevent the sugarpaste crusting over.

Cakes

Protect your cake by placing it in a clean, covered cardboard cake box, and store somewhere cool and dry, but never in a refrigerator. If the box is slightly larger than the cake and the cake is to be transported, use non-slip matting to prevent the cake moving.

Cupcakes

Store cooled cupcakes in an airtight container at room temperature until you are ready to decorate them. Decorate your cakes as close as possible to when they will be eaten to help prevent the cakes drying out. If this is not possible, use foil or high-quality greaseproof cases and cover the whole of the top of each cake to help seal in the moisture.

Cardboard cupcake boxes are the best way to transport cupcakes – they are simply boxes with an insert, which prevents the cakes from sliding. You can stack the boxes so the cupcakes are easy to carry. Boxes are available for the different case sizes and range from single-hole boxes to at least 24 holes.

Cookies

Cookies keep remarkably well, so you can bake and decorate them well in advance. Once decorated and dried, I like to place my cookies in cookie bags to protect them. However if you have lots to store, allow all the icing and decoration to dry and then store in airtight containers, layering them with kitchen paper.

Mini-cakes

A nice way to protect your mini-cakes is to pop them into little PVC cubes; this way they can be displayed and stacked at the same time.

Suppliers

Lindy's Cakes Ltd (LC)

Unit 2, Station Approach, Wendover
Buckinghamshire HP22 6BN
Tel: +44 (0)1296 622418
www.lindyscakes.co.uk
Online shop for products and
equipment used in this and Lindy's
other books, including Lindy's own
ranges of cutters and stencils

Abbreviations used in this booklet

DS – Designer Stencils

FMM – FMM Sugarcraft

GI – Great Impressions

HP – Holly Products

LC – Lindy's Cakes Ltd

PC – Patchwork Cutters

PME – PME Sugarcraft

SK – Squires Kitchen

UK

Alan Silverwood Ltd

Ledsam House, Ledsam Street
Birmingham B16 8DN
Tel: +44 (0)121 454 3571
www.alansilverwood.co.uk
Manufacturer of multi-sized cake
pan, multi mini cake pans and
spherical moulds/ball tins

Ceefor Cakes

PO Box 443, Leighton Buzzard
Bedfordshire LU7 1AJ
Tel: +44 (0)1525 375237
www.ceeforcakes.co.uk
Supplier of strong cake boxes –
most sizes available

FMM Sugarcraft (FMM)

Unit 7, Chancerygate Business
Park, Whiteleaf Road,
Hemel Hempstead, Hertfordshire
HP3 9HD
Tel: +44 (0)1442 292970
www.fmmsugarcraft.com
Manufacturer of cutters

Holly Products (HP)

Primrose Cottage, Church Walk,
Norton in Hales
Shropshire, TF9 4QX
Tel: +44 (0)1630 655759
www.hollyproducts.co.uk
Manufacturer and supplier of
embossing sticks and moulds

M&B Specialised Confectioners Ltd

3a Millmead Estate, Mill Mead
Road
London N17 9ND
Tel: +44 (0)208 801 7948
www.mbsc.co.uk
Manufacturer and supplier of
sugarpaste

Patchwork Cutters (PC)

Unit 12, Arrowe Commercial Park,
Arrowe Brook Road, Upton
Wirral CH49 1AB
Tel: +44 (0)151 678 5053
www.patchworkcutters.co.uk
Manufacturer and supplier of
cutters and embossers

US

Global Sugar Art

625 Route 3, Unit 3
Plattsburgh, NY 12901
Tel: 1-518-561-3039 or 1-800-420-6088 (toll
free)
www.globalsugarart.com
Sugarcraft supplier that imports many UK
products to the US

Cake Craft Shoppe

3530 Highway 6
Sugar Land, TX 77478
Tel: 1-281-491-3920
www.cakecraftshoppe.com
Sugarcraft supplier

First Impressions Molds

300 Business Park Way, Suite A-200
Royal Palm Beach, FL 33411
Tel: 1-561-784-7186
www.firstimpressionsmolds.com
Manufacturer and supplier of moulds

Australia

Iced Affair

53 Church Street
Camperdown NSW 2050
Tel: +61 (0)2 9519 3679
www.icedaffair.com.au
Sugarcraft supplier